QUOTES AND MIRACLES OF JESUS CHRIST

PALMETTO

PUBLISHING

Charleston, SC
www.PalmettoPublishing.com

Hardcover ISBN: 9798822967175
Paperback ISBN: 9798822967182
eBook ISBN: 9798822967199

QUOTES AND MIRACLES OF JESUS CHRIST

NORBERT J. HORNEK

CONTENTS

JESUS OWN WORDS   1

CHAPTER 1 - JESUS CHRIST IN HIS OWN WORDS   3

CHAPTER 2 – JESUS BUILDS HIS CHURCH   7

Eucharist	Two Masters
Baptizing	Marriage
The Ten Commandments Anger	
Adultery	An eye for an eye

CHAPTER 3 - MY BODY, MY SOUL, MY CHOICE   19

The road to Hell	Abortion
Homosexuality	Same sex marriage,
The End Will Come	Praying
Rewards	Justice
Faith Alone religion	All transgender activity
Rapture religion	Those that mislead you

WHO IS NORBERT J. HORNEK?   70

JESUS OWN WORDS

This book was created and published for our family however, if you think this book can help you save your own soul and the souls of your love ones then this book is for you too.

The average life spam of a person is about eighty years old. So subtract your age from eighty and your answer is how many years your body have left on this earth, that is if your body lives to be eighty years old.

Obviously, if you have an accident, if you are murdered, develop cancer, have a heart attack or any thing that will take your life, then the years left for your body will be less on this earth and your soul will be judge by Jesus unless you go straight to Heaven, you won't be judge.

If you look at the summary page you will find subject matters that will draw your interest. Jesus in His own words will let you know His will and the will of the Father.

When your body dies and your soul enters eternity, Jesus will or will not judge you based on the condition of you soul. Your soul will have only itself and all of your money and power will go to someone else.

This book has actual quotes of Jesus and His miracles that were recorded. While you are still alive you will have to make a decision to do God's will or not to do his will. At lease by reading this book you will know what God's will is.

If you do God's will, your soul will live with God forever. If you don't do God's will, your soul will live with Satan forever.

Now when evening had come, Jesus was reclining at the table with the twelve disciples. As they were eating and Jesus said, "Most certainly I tell you that one of you will betray me."

They were exceedingly sorrowful, and each began to ask him, "It isn't me is it Lord?" He answered, "He who dipped his hand with me in the dish will betray me.

The Son of Man goes even as it is written of him but woe to that man whom the Son of Man is betrayed! It would be better for that man if he wasn't born." **Matthew 26:20-24**

CHAPTER 1 – JESUS CHRIST IN HIS OWN WORDS

A voice came out of the cloud saying, "This is my beloved Son. Listen to him!" When they heard the voice Jesus was found alone. They were silent. **Luke 9:35,36**

They said to Jesus, "What must we do, that we may work the works of God?"

Jesus answered them, "This is the work of God, that you believe me whom God has sent." **John 6:28,29**

Jesus said, "You shall be perfect just as your Father in heaven is perfect." **Matthew 5:48**

Jesus said, "All things have been delivered to me by my Father. No one knows the Son except the Father. Nor does anyone know the Father except the Son." **Matthew 11:27**

Jesus said, for God so loved the world that he gave his only Son. Whoever believes in him will not perish and have eternal life. For God didn't send his Son into the world to judge the world but that the world should be saved through him." **John 3:16,17**

After six days Jesus took Peter, James, John and his brother and brought them up into a high mountain by themselves. He was changed before them. His face shone like the sun and his garments became as white as the light. Moses and Elijah talking with Jesus appeared to them.

Peter answered and said to Jesus, "Lord it is good for us to be here. Let's make three tents, one for you, one for Moses and one for Elijah."

While Peter was still speaking a bright cloud overshadowed them and voice came out of the cloud saying, "This is my beloved Son in whom I am well pleased. Listen to him."

When the disciples heard this they fell on the ground and were afraid. Jesus came and touched them and said, "Get up and don't be afraid." Lifting up their eyes they saw no one except Jesus. **Matthew 17:1-8**

Jesus said, "For as the Father has life in himself also he gave to the Son life in himself. The Father gave the Son authority to execute judgment. Don't marvel at this for the hour will come in which all who are in the tombs will hear his voice and will come out. Those who have done good to the resurrection of life and those who have done evil to the resurrection of judgment. As I hear I judge and my judgment is righteous because I don't seek my own will but the will of my Father who sent me."
John 5:26-30

Jesus said to him, "I am the way the truth and the life. No one comes to the Father except through me. If you known me, you know my Father. From now on you know him and have seen him."
John 14:6,7

Jesus said, "He who loves his father or mother more than me is not worthy of me and he who loves his son or daughter more than me isn't worthy of me. He who doesn't take his cross and follow me isn't worthy of me. He who seeks his life will lose it and he who loses his life for my sake will find it."**Matthew 10:37-39**

Jesus said, "He that is not with me is against me. He who doesn't gather with me scatters." **Luke 11:23**

Jesus said, "Anyone who confesses me before men, I will confess him before my Father who is in heaven. But whoever denies me before men, I will deny him before my Father who is in heaven." **Matthew 10:32,33**

Jesus said to all, "If anyone desires to come after me, he must deny himself, take up his cross and follow me. For whoever desires to save his life will lose it and whoever will lose his life for my sake will save it." **Luke 9:23,24**

Jesus said, "Even as the Father has loved me, I also have loved you. If you keep my commandments you will remain in my love even as I have kept my Father's commandments and remain in his love." **John 15:9,10**

Jesus said, "All those whom the Father gives me, will come to me. He who comes to me I will in no way throw out. For I have come down from heaven, not to do my will but the will of the one who sent me. This is the will of my Father who sent me. All those he has given to me will lose nothing and I will raise them up on the last day. This is the will of the one who sent me. Everyone who sees the Son and believes in him will have eternal life and I will raise him up on the last day." **John 6:37-40**

Jesus said, "Most certainly, I tell you if a person keeps my word he will never see death." **John 8:51**

Jesus said, "If you remain in me and my words remain in you then whatever you desire will be done for you." **John 15:7**

Jesus said, "Most certainly I tell you, he who hears my word and believes the Father who sent me has eternal life and doesn't come into judgment, but has passed out of death into life."
John 5:24

Jesus entered into a boat with his disciples and said to them, "Let's go over to the other side of the lake." So they launched out. As they sailed, he fell asleep. A wind storm came down on the lake and they were taking on dangerous amounts of water.

They came to him and awoke him up saying, "Master, master, we are dying!"

He awoke rebuked the wind and the raging waters ceased and it became calm. Jesus said to them, "Where is your faith?"

Being afraid they said to one another, "Who is Jesus, that the wind and the water obey him?" **Luke 8:22-25**

Jesus called the twelve and he said to them, "If any man wants to be first he shall be last of all and servant of all." **Mark 9:35**

CHAPTER 2 – JESUS BUILDS HIS CHURCH

When Jesus came to the region of Caesarea Philippi, he asked his disciples, "Who do people say the Son of Man is?"

They replied, "Some say John the Baptist others say Elijah and still others Jeremiah or one of the prophets."

"But what about you?" he asked. "Who do you say I am?"

Simon answered, "You are the Messiah, the Son of the living God."

Jesus replied, "Blessed are you Simon son of Jonah for this was not revealed to you by flesh and blood but by my Father in heaven.

I tell you that you are Peter and on this rock I will build my church and the gates of Hell will not overcome it. I will give you the keys to the kingdom of heaven whatever you bind on earth will be bound in heaven and whatever you loose on earth will be loose in heaven." Then he ordered his disciples not to tell anyone that he was the Messiah. **Matthew 16:13-20**

Jesus said, "You did not choose me, but I chose you and appointed you so that you might go and bear fruit that will last. Whatever you ask in my name the Father will give you. This is my command, love each other. **John 15:16,17**

Jesus said, "You are the light of the world. A town built on a hill cannot be hidden. Neither do people light a lamp and put it under a bowl. Instead they put it on its stand and it gives light to everyone in the house. In the same way let your light shine before others that they may see your good deeds and glorify your Father in heaven." **Matthew 5:14-16**

Jesus called the crowd to him along with his disciples and said, "Whoever wants to be my disciple must deny themselves and take up their cross and follow me. For whoever wants to save their life will lose it but whoever loses their life for me and for the gospel will save it. What good is it for someone to gain the whole world and forfeit their soul?

If anyone is ashamed of me and my words in this adulterous and sinful generation the Son of Man will be ashamed of them when they comes in his Father's glory with the holy angels."
Mark 8:34-38

Jesus therefore said to those Jews who had believed him, "If you remain in my word then you are truly my disciples. You will know the truth and the truth will set you free."

They answered him, "We are Abraham's offspring and have never been in bondage to anyone. Why do you say, You will be made free?"

Jesus answered them, Everyone who commits a sin is the servant of that sin." **John 8:31-34**

Eucharist - Jesus said to them, "Most certainly I tell you, unless you eat the flesh of the Son of Man and drink his blood, you don't have life in yourselves. He who eats my flesh and drinks my blood has eternal life and I will raise him up on the last day. For my flesh is food and my blood is drink. He who eats my flesh and drinks my blood lives in me and I in him. As the Father sent me and I live because of the Father. He who feeds on me will live because of me. I am the bread that came down out of heaven, not as our fathers ate the manna and died. He who eats this bread will live forever."

He said these things in the synagogue, as he taught in Capernaum. When many of the disciples heard this they said. "This is hard to believe. Who can listen to it?"

But Jesus knowing that his disciples murmured at this said to them, "Does this cause you to stumble? Then what if you would see the Son of Man ascending to where he was before? It is the spirit who gives life. The flesh profits nothing. The words that I speak to you are spirit and are life.

But there are some of you who don't believe." For Jesus knew from the beginning who they were that don't believe and who it was who would betray him. He said, "I have said to you that no one can come to me, unless he is given to me by my Father."

At this, many of his disciples went back, and walked no more with him.

Jesus said therefore to the twelve, "Are you going to leave too?"

Peter answered him, "Lord, to whom would we go? You have the words of eternal life. We have come to believe and know that you are the Christ, the Son of the living God."
John 6:59-69

Jesus said to them, "Most certainly I tell you, it wasn't Moses who gave you the bread out of heaven but my Father gives you the true bread out of heaven. For the bread of God is that which comes down out of heaven and gives life to the world."

They said, "Lord, always give us this bread."

Jesus said to them, "I am the bread of life. Whoever comes to me will not be hungry and whoever believes in me will never be thirsty. But I told you that you have seen me and yet you don't believe. All those whom the Father gives me will come to me. He who comes to me I will in no way throw out. For I have come down from heaven, not to do my own will but the will of him who sent me. This is the will of my Father who sent me, that of all he has given me I should lose nothing but should raise him up on the last day. This is the will of the one who sent me that everyone who sees the Son and believes in him will have eternal life and I will raise him up on the last day." **John 6:32-40**

Jesus said, "I am the living bread which came down out of heaven. If anyone eats of this bread will live forever. Yes, the bread which I will give for the life of the world is my flesh."

The Jews said, "How can this man give us his flesh to eat?"
As they were eating Jesus took bread and blessed and broke it saying, "Take and eat. This is my body." He took the cup and when he had given thanks he gave the cup to them. They all drank of it. He said to them, "This is my blood of the new covenant which is poured out for many."

Jesus said, "Most certainly I tell you, I will not drink of the fruit of the vine until the day when I drink it anew in God's Kingdom." When they had sung a hymn, they went out to the Mount of Olives." **Mark 14:22-26**

Jesus took bread and when he had given thanks, he broke and gave it to them saying, "This is my body which is given up for you. Do this in memory of me." Likewise, he took the cup after supper saying, "This cup is the new covenant in my blood which is poured out for you." **Luke 22:19,20**

Jesus said, "You search the Scriptures because you think that in them you have eternal life because these Scriptures testify about me. Yet you will not come to me that you may have life. I know you and you don't have God's love in yourselves. I have come in my Father's name and you don't receive me. If another comes in his own name you will receive him. How can you give glory to one another and you don't seek glory that comes from God?

The Father is one who accuses you not Moses. You have set your hopes on Moses. For if you believed Moses you would believe me. Moses wrote about me. But if you don't believe his writings how will you believe my words?" **John 5:39-47**

"If you stand before others and are willing to say you believe me then I will tell my Father in heaven that you belong to me. But if you stand before others and say you do not believe me then I will tell my Father in heaven that you do not belong to me." **Matthew 10:32,33**

BAPTIZING - When Jesus was baptized he came out of the water and the heavens opened up. He saw the Spirit of God descending as a dove coming down upon him. A voice out of the heavens said, "This is my beloved Son with whom I am well pleased." **Matthew 3:16,17**

Jesus said to them, "Go into all the world and preach the Good News to the whole creation. He who believes and is baptized will be saved. Those who don't believe will be condemned. These signs will accompany those who believe. In my name they will cast out demons. They will speak with new languages. They will take up serpents and if they drink any deadly thing it won't hurt them. They will lay hands on the sick and the sick will recover."

After the Lord had spoken to them they went out and preached everywhere. **Mark 16:15-20**

But the eleven disciples went into Galilee to the mountain where Jesus had sent them. When they saw him they bowed down to him but some didn't believe.

Jesus came to them and spoke to them saying, "All authority has been given to me in heaven and on earth. Go and make disciples of all nations baptizing them in the name of the Father and of the Son and of the Holy Spirit teaching them to observe all things that I commanded you. I am with you even to the end of time." **Matthew 28:16-20**

Now there was a man of the Pharisees named Nicodemus, a ruler of the Jews. He came to Jesus by night and said to him. "Rabbi we know that you are a teacher from God for no one can do these signs that you do unless God is with him.

"Jesus answered him, "I tell you, unless one is born anew he won't enter God's Kingdom."

Nicodemus said to him, "How can a man be born when he is old? Can he enter a second time into his mother's womb and be born again?"

Jesus answered, "Most certainly I tell you, unless one is born of water and spirit he can't enter into God's Kingdom. That which is born of the flesh is flesh. That which is born of the Spirit is spirit. Don't marvel that I said to you 'You must be born anew.' The wind blows where it wants to and you hear its sound but don't know where it comes from and where it is going. So is everyone who is born of the Spirit."

Nicodemus answered him, "How can this be?"

Jesus answered him, "Are you the teacher of Israel and don't understand these things? Most certainly I tell you we speak that which we know and testify of that which we have seen and you don't understand. If I told you earthly things and you don't believe how will you believe me if I tell you heavenly things? No one has ascended into heaven but the Son of Man who is in Heaven has descended out of heaven. As Moses lifted up the serpent in the wilderness even so must the Son of Man be lifted up that whoever believes in him will not perish but have eternal life.

For God so loved the world, that he gave his only Son that whoever believes in him should not perish but have eternal life. For God didn't send his Son into the world to judge the world but that the world will be saved through him. He who believes in him will not be judged. Those who don't believe has all ready been judged. Because they don't believed in the Son of God. This is the judgment that the light has come into the world and men who's works are evil, loved the darkness rather than the light. For everyone who does evil hates the light because his works would be exposed. He who knows the truth comes to the light so that his works may be revealed. Their good works have been achieve with God."

Jesus came with his disciples into the land of Judea. He stayed there with them and they baptized many people. John the Baptize was not yet thrown in prison and he was baptizing in Enon near Salim. The people came and were baptized. A dispute arose on the part of John's disciples with some Jews about purification.

They came to John and said to him, "Rabbi, the one that you   told us about is baptizing many people."

John answered, "A man can receive nothing unless it has been given him from heaven. You yourselves testify that I said, 'I am not the Christ' but I have been sent before him." **John 3:1-28**

MARRIAGE - Jesus said, "But at the beginning of creation God made them male and female. For this reason a man will leave his father and mother and be united to his wife. The two will become one Jesus said, For there is no good tree that produces
rotten fruit nor a rotten tree that produces good fruit. For each tree is known by its own fruit.

For people don't gather figs from thorns nor do they gather grapes from a bramble bush. The good man out of the good treasure of his heart brings out that which is good and the evil man out of the evil treasure of his heart brings out that which is evil for out of the abundance of his heart his mouth speaks." So they are no longer two but one flesh. What God has joined together let no one separate." **Mark 10:6-9, Luke 6:43,44**

The third day, there was a wedding in Cana of Galilee. The mother of Jesus was there. Jesus with his disciples were invited to the wedding. When the wine ran out, Jesus' mother said to him, "They have no wine."

Jesus said to her, "Woman, what does that have to do with you and me? My hour has not yet come."

His mother said to the servants, "Whatever he says to you, do it."

Now there were six water pots of stone set there after the Jews way of purifying containing two or three metretes apiece. Jesus said to them. "Fill the water pots with water." So they filled them up to the brim. He said to them. "Now draw some out and take it to the head of the feast." When the head of the feast tasted the water that has become wine. He didn't know where the wine came from but the servants who had drawn the water knew.

The head of the feast called the bridegroom and said to him. "Everyone serves the good wine first and when the guests have drunk freely then the wine that is not as good is served. You have kept the good wine until now!" This beginning of his signs Jesus did in Cana of Galilee and revealed his glory then his disciples believed in him. **John 2:1-11**

THE TEN COMMANDMENTS - When the Pharisees heard that Jesus had silenced the Sadducee's and then they gathered themselves together. A lawyer, testing him asked him a question. "Teacher, which is the greatest commandment?"

Jesus said to him, "You shall love the Lord your God with all your heart, with all your soul, and with all your mind. This is the first and greatest commandment. A second likewise is this, You shall love your neighbor as yourself. The whole law and the prophets depend on these two commandments." **Matthew 22:34-40**

Jesus said, "If you love me, keep my commandments."
John 14:15

ANGER - Jesus said, "You have heard that it was said to the ancient ones, 'You shall not murder;' and 'whoever murders will be in danger of the judgment.' But I tell you that everyone who is angry with his brother without a cause will be in danger of judgment. Whoever says to his brother, 'You Fool!' will be in danger of the council. But saying, 'You fool!' will be in danger of the fire of Hell."
Matthew 5:21,22

Jesus said, "You have heard that it was said, 'You shall love your neighbor and hate your enemy.' But I tell you, love your enemies, bless those who curse you, do good to those who hate you and pray for those who mistreat you and persecute you, that you

may be children of your Father who is in heaven. For he makes his sun to rise on the evil and the good and sends rain on the just and the unjust. For if you love those who love you, what reward do you have? Don't even the tax collectors do the same?If you only greet your friends, what more do you do to others? Don't even the tax collectors do the same? You shall be perfect just as your Father in heaven is perfect." **Matthew 5:43-48**

ADULTERY - Jesus said, "You have heard that it was said, 'You shall not commit adultery' but I tell you that everyone who gazes at a woman for lust after her has committed adultery with her already in his heart. If your right eye causes you to stumble, pluck it out and throw it away. For it is more profitable for you that one of your members should perish than for your whole body to be cast into Hell. If your right hand causes you to stumble, cut it off and throw it away. For it is more profitable for you that one of your members should perish than for your whole body to be cast into Hell." **Matthew 5:27-30**

AN EYE FOR AN EYE - Jesus said, "You have heard that it was said, 'An eye for an eye, and a tooth for a tooth.' But I tell you, don't resist him who is evil but whoever strikes you on your right cheek, also turn to him the other cheek. If anyone sues you to take away your coat, also let him have your cloak too. Whoever compels you to go one mile, go two miles. Don't turn away a person who wants to borrow from you." **Matthew 5:38-42**

Jesus said, "Forgive those who trespasses and your heavenly Father will forgive you. But if you don't forgive those their trespasses, neither will your Father forgive your trespasses." **Matthew 6:14,15**

TWO MASTERS - Jesus said, "No one can serve two masters. Either you will hate the one and love the other or you will be devoted to the one and despise the other. You cannot serve both God and money." **Matthew 6:24**

"Teacher," he declared. "Since I was a boy I have kept all of the commandments. Jesus looked at him and loved him."

Jesus said, "One thing you lack. Go sell everything you have and give it to the poor. Then come and follow me and you will have treasure in heaven." The man went away sad because he was very wealthy."

Jesus looked around and said to his disciples, "How hard it is for the rich to enter the kingdom of God!" The disciples were amazed at his words.

But Jesus said again, "Children it is hard to enter the kingdom of God. It is a lot easier for a camel to go through the eye of a needle than for someone who is rich to enter the kingdom of God." The disciples were even more amazed. They said to each other, "Who can be saved?" Jesus looked at them and said." With man this is impossible but with God all things are possible." **Mark 10:20-27**

Jesus said, "Do not store up for yourselves treasures on earth where moths and vermin destroy and where thieves break in and steal. But store up for yourselves treasures in heaven where moths and vermin do not destroy and where thieves do not break in and steal. For where your treasure is there your heart will also be." **Matthew 6:19-21**

Jesus spoke a parable to them. "Can the blind guide the blind? Won't they both fall into a pit? A disciple is not above his teacher but everyone when he is fully trained will be like his teacher." **Luke 6:39,40**

Jesus said, "Why do you see the speck of chaff that is in your brother's eye but don't consider the beam that is in your own eye? How can you tell your brother, brother let me remove the speck of chaff that is in your eye, when you yourself don't see the beam that is in your own eye? You hypocrite! First remove the beam from your own eye and then you will be able to see clearly and remove the speck of chaff that is in your brother's eye." **Luke 6:41,42**

Jesus said, "For there is no good tree that produces rotten fruit nor a rotten tree that produces good fruit. For each tree is known by its own fruit. For people don't gather figs from thorns nor do they gather grapes from a bramble bush. The good man out of the good treasure of his heart brings out that which is good and the evil man out of the evil treasure of his heart brings out that which is evil because for out of the abundance of his heart his mouth speaks." **Luke 6:43,44**

Jesus said, "Moreover when you fast don't be like the hypocrites with sad faces. For they disfigure their faces that they may be seen by men to be fasting. Most certainly I tell you they have received their reward. But when you fast anoint your head and wash your face so that you are not seen by men to be fasting but only by your Father who sees you in secret will reward you." **Matthew 6:16-18**

Then Peter came and said to him, "Lord, how often shall I forgive my brother who keeps sinning against me? Should I forgive him seven times?"
Jesus said to him, "I tell you not seven times but seventy times seven." **Matthew 18:21,22**

CHAPTER 3 – MY BODY, MY SOUL, MY CHOICE

Jesus said, While virgins went away to buy candles the bridegroom came and those who were ready went in with him to the wedding feast and the door was shut.

Afterward other virgins came saying, "Lord, Lord, open the door."

But he answered, "Most certainly I tell you I don't know you."

Jesus said, "Watch for you don't know the day nor the hour in which the Son of Man is coming for you." **Mathew 25:10-13**

Jesus said, "But no one knows of that day and hour not even the angels of heaven but only my Father."

Jesus said, "As the days of Noah were so will the coming of the Son of Man. Before the flood they were eating and drinking marrying and giving in marriage. Then Noah entered the ship and they didn't know until the flood came and took them all away.

So will the coming of the Son of Man. Two men will be in the field one will be taken and one will be left. Two women will be grinding

at the mill one will be taken and one will be left. Watch, for you don't know what hour your Lord is coming for you."
Matthew 24:36-42

Jesus said, "But of that day or that hour no one knows, not even the angels in heaven, nor the Son but only the Father. Watch keep alert and pray for you don't know when it's your time." **Mark 13:32,33**

The LORD declares, for those who honor me I will honor them and those who don't honor me shall be lightly honor.

1Samuel 2:30

Jesus said, "If you stand before others and are willing to say you believe in me then I will tell my Father in heaven that you belong to me. But if you stand before others and say you do not believe in me then I will tell my Father in heaven that you don't belong to me. **Matthew 10:32,33**

THE ROAD TO HELL - If you don't believe in the Eucharist, you are on the road to Hell.

If you don't received Holy Communion regularly, you are on the road to Hell.

If you believe that all you have to do to enter Heaven is to have "Faith Only" in God. You are on the road to Hell.

If you believe in "Rapture," you are on the road to Hell.

If you don't show respect to the Eucharist at Mass by wearing jeans, shorts, tennis shoes, slippers, supporting a sport team on your shirt in the House of God, you are on the road to Hell.

If you are showing bad example by not respecting the Eucharist in the House of God and you don't correct yourself and in your family, you are on the road to Hell.

If you don't believe Jesus words, you are on the road to Hell.

If you don't have your children baptize, you are on the road to Hell. If you are stealing from others, you are on the road to Hell.

If you hate certain people, other religion, other countries, you are on the road to Hell.

If you don't believe in going to confession, you are on the road to Hell.

If you don' believe in Confirmation, you are on the road to Hell.

If you don't take your religion seriously, you are on the road to Hell.

If you don't believe every statement Jesus says, you are on the road to Hell.

If your number one priority in your life is your career or your family or your money or your favorite sport team or your animals or your garden or your vacation trips and it's not God, you are on the road to Hell.

If two people living together and are not married as man and wife, you are on the road to Hell.

If you think that you can keep sinning and be save by the prayers of the sick, you are on the road to Hell. God know your thoughts and He may allow an accident happen to you on the interstate or a heart attack and there won't be a priest around to pray the prayers of the sick for you.

If you are practicing any transgender activity, you are on the road to Hell.

If you are practicing Homosexuality, you are on the road to Hell.

If you are in a same sex marriage, you are on the road to Hell.

If you believe in Bisexual, you are on the road to Hell.

If you believe in Pan sexuality, you are on the road to Hell.

If the Catholic Church doesn't recognize your marriage as a marriage, you are on the road to Hell.

If you don't have your children baptize, you are on the road to Hell.

If You believe in murdering a baby in the wound, you are on the road to Hell.

If you believe in murdering a person that is outside the wound or assist suicide, you are on the road to Hell.

If you believe in abortion, you are on the road to Hell.

If you believe in Lesbian, you are on the road to Hell.

If you don't believe Jesus words, you are on the road to Hell.

If you don't try to save your soul, you are on the road to Hell.

Watch, for you don't know in what hour Our Lord is coming." **Matthew 24:42**

Jesus said, that Hell is a place where you are cast into the fire of Hell where the fire will never be quenched and where your body will not die. Mark 9:43-48

Jesus said,The Son of Man goes even as it is written of him but woe to that man whom the Son of Man is betrayed! It would be better for that man if he wasn't born."Matthew 26:20-24

You are on the road to Hell means currently you are headed in the direction of Hell. If you don't stop what you are doing you will end up in Hell.

Don't you think that it's about time that you get off this road to Hell and get on the road to Heaven before something bad happens to you.

THE END WILL COME. - Jesus went out from the temple and was going on his way. His disciples came to him to show him the buildings of the temple.

Jesus answered them, "You see all of these things, don't you? Most certainly I tell you, there will won"t be a stone left on another stone that will not be thrown down."

As Jesus was sitting on the Mount of Olives, the disciples came to him privately saying, "Tell us, when will these things will happen? What is the sign of your coming at the end of time?"

Jesus answered them, "Be careful that no one leads you astray. For many will come in my name saying. "I am the Christ and he will lead many astray. You will hear of wars and rumors of wars. See that you aren't troubled for all this must happen for the end is not now."

Jesus continued, "For nation will rise against nation and kingdom against kingdom and there will be famines, plagues and earthquakes in various places. But all these things are the beginning of birth pains."

Jesus said, they will deliver you up to oppression and will kill you. You will be hated by all of the nations for my name's sake. Then many will stumble and will deliver up one another and hate one another.

Many false prophets will arise and will lead many astray. Because iniquity will be multiplied, the love of many will grow cold. But he who endures to the end will be saved.

This Good News of the Kingdom will be preached in the whole world for a testimony to all the nations and then the end will come."

Jesus continued, "When, you see the abomination of desolation, which was spoken of through Daniel the prophet, standing in the holy place letting those who are in Judea flee to the mountains."

Jesus said, don't Let the one who are on the housetop go down to take out the things that are in his house. Don't let those who are in the field to return back to get their clothes. But woe to those who are with child and and nursing mothers for it will be hard on them."

Jesus said, pray that your flight will not be in the winter nor on a Sabbath, for there will be great suffering, such as has not been from the beginning of the world until now nor will ever be.

Unless those days had been shortened, no flesh would have been saved. But for the sake of the chosen ones, those days will be shortened.

If any man tells you, 'Behold, here is the Christ!' or, 'There!' don't believe it. For there will be false christs, and false prophets, and they will show great signs and wonders, so as to lead you astray, even the chosen ones. I have told you beforehand. If they tell you, he is in the wilderness, don't go out or he is in the inner rooms, don't believe it. For as the lightning flashes from the east and is seen even to the west, so will the coming of the Son of Man be. For wherever the carcass are, that is where the vultures will gather. But immediately after the suffering of those days the sun will be darkened, the moon won't give its light, the stars will fall from the sky and the powers of the heavens will be shaken and then the sign of the Son of Man will appear in the sky. Then all the tribes of the earth will be happy because they will see the Son of Man coming on the clouds of the sky with power and great glory. He will send out his angels with a great sound of a trumpet and they will gather together his chosen ones from the four winds, from one end of the sky to the other."

Jesus continues, "Now from the fig tree learn this parable. When fig tree branch has now become tender and produces its leaves, you know that the summer is near. When you see all these things, you know that Jesus is near even at your door."

Most certainly I tell you, "This generation will not pass away until all these things happen. Heaven and earth will pass away, but my words will not pass away. But no one knows of that day and hour, not even the angels of heaven except my Father will know."

Jesus continues, "As the days of Noah were, so will the coming of the Son of Man. For as in those days which were before the flood they were eating and drinking, marrying and giving in marriage, until the day that Noah entered into the ship and they didn't know until the flood came and took them all away. So will the coming of the Son of Man.

Then two men will be in the field, one will be taken and one will be left. Two women will be grinding at the mill, one will be taken and one will be left. Watch for you don't know in what hour your Lord comes. But know this, that if the master of the house had known in what watch of the night the thief was coming, he would have watched and would not have allowed his house to be broken into. Be ready, within an hour, that you don't expect it the Son of Man will come."

Jesus said, "Who is the faithful and wise servant, whom his lord has watch over his household? Blessed is that servant whom his lord finds doing so when he comes. Most certainly I tell you that he will set him over all that he has. But if that evil servant should say in his heart, 'My lord is delaying his coming,' and begins to beat his fellow servants and eat and drink with the drunkards, the lord of that servant will come in a day when he doesn't expect it and in an hour when he doesn't know it and will cut him in pieces and appoint his portion with the hypocrites in Hell. That is where the weeping and grinding of teeth will be." **Matthew 24:1-51**

Jesus said, "Enter in by the narrow gate for the gate is wide and the way is broad that leads to destruction and there are many who enter by it and they will find death.

The gate that is narrow and the way is restricted that leads to life! They are the ones who find life." **Matthew 7:13,14**

Jesus said to his disciples, "Most certainly I say to you, a rich man will enter into the Kingdom of Heaven with difficulty. Again I tell
you that it is easier for a camel to go through a needle's eye than for a rich man to enter into God's Kingdom."

When the disciples heard it, they were exceedingly astonished, saying, "Who then can be saved?"

Looking at them Jesus said, "With men this is impossible but with God all things are possible." **Matthew 19:23-26**

Jesus said, "Not everyone who says to me, 'Lord, Lord,' will enter into the Kingdom of Heaven, but he who does the will of my Father will enter into heaven." **Matthew 7:21**

When it was evening he came with the twelve. As they sat and were eating, Jesus said, "Most certainly I tell you, one of you will betray me, he who eats with me."

They began to be sorrowful, and to ask him one by one, "Surely not I?" And others said, the same?

Jesus answered them, "It is one of the twelve, he who dips with me in the dish. For the Son of Man goes, even as it is written about him but woe to that man by whom the Son of Man is betrayed. It would be better for that man if he had not been born." **Mark 14:17-21**

Jesus said, "Don't be afraid of those who kill the body and are not able to kill the soul. Rather fear the one who is able to destroy both the body and the soul." **Matthew 10:28**

Jesus said, "If your hand causes you to stumble cut it off. It is better for you to enter into God's Kingdom rather than having your two hands cast into the fire of Hell where the fire is not quenched and where their bodies will not die.

If your foot causes you to stumble cut it off. It is better for you to enter into God's Kingdom rather than having your two feet to be cast into the fire of Hell where the fire will never be quenched and where their bodies will not die.

If your eye causes you to stumble cast it out. It is better for you to enter into God's Kingdom rather than having two eyes to be cast into hell where the fire is not quenched and where their bodies will not die." **Mark 9:43-48**

Jesus said, "Whoever will cause one of these little ones who believe in me to stumble it would be better for him if he were thrown into the sea with a millstone hung around his neck."
Mark 9:42

Now when evening came Jesus was reclining at the table with the twelve disciples. As they were eating he said, "Most certainly I tell you that one of you will betray me."

They were exceedingly sorrowful, and each began to ask him, "It isn't me, is it, Lord?"

Jesus answered, "He who dipped his hand with me in the dish will betray me. The Son of Man goes even as it is written of him, but woe to that man through whom the Son of Man is betrayed. It would be better for that man if he had not been born."

Judas, who betrayed him answered, "It isn't me is it Rabbi?"
Jesus said to him, "You said it." **Matthew 26:20-24**

Jesus said, "Woe to you who are rich! For you have received your reward. Woe to you who are full now, for you will be hungry. Woe to you who laugh now, for you will mourn and weep. Woe when men speak well of you, for their fathers did the same thing to the false prophets." **Luke 6:24-26**

Jesus said, "But of that day or that hour no one knows not even the angels in heave nor the Son but only the Father. Stay alert and pray for you don't know when it's your time."
Mark 13:32,33

PRAYING - Jesus said, "Ask, and it will be given you. Seek and you will find. Knock and it will be opened for you. For everyone who asks receives. He who seeks finds. To him who knocks it will be opened. Is there anyone of you would give his son a stone if he asks for bread? If he asks for a fish would you give him a

serpent? If you know how to give good gifts to your children, how much more will your Father who is in heaven give good things to those who ask him! Whatever you desire for men to do for you, you should also do for them for this is the law and the prophets."
Matthew 7:7-12

Jesus said, "In praying, don't use vain repetitions as the Gentiles do, for they think that they will be heard for their much speaking. Don't be like them, for your Father knows what things you need before you ask him. Pray like this:

'Our Father in heaven, may your name be kept holy. Let your Kingdom come. Let your will be done on earth as it is in heaven. Give us today our daily bread. Forgive us our debts, as we also forgive our debtors. Bring us not into temptation, but deliver us from the evil one. For yours is the Kingdom, the power and the glory forever. Amen.'

For if you forgive men their trespasses, your heavenly Father will also forgive you. But if you don't forgive men their trespasses, neither will your Father forgive your trespasses."
Matthew 6:7-15

Jesus said, "When you pray, you shall not be as the hypocrites, for they love to stand and pray in the synagogues and in the corners of the streets, that they may be seen by men. Most certainly, I tell you, they have received their reward. But when you pray, enter into your inner room, and having shut your door, pray to your Father who is in secret and your Father who sees you in secret will reward you openly. In praying, don't use
vain repetitions as the Gentiles do, for they think that they will be heard for their speaking. Don't be like them, for your Father knows what things you need before you ask him."**Matthew 6:5-8**

JESUS PRAYS - Jesus had been baptized and was praying. The sky was opened and the Holy Spirit descended in a bodily

form like a dove on him and a voice came out of the sky saying, "You are my beloved Son. In you I am well pleased." Luke 3:21,22

Early in the morning, while it was still dark Jesus rose up and went out into a deserted area and prayed. Simon and others searched for him. They found him and told him, "Everyone is looking for you."
Mark 1:35,36

The report concerning him spread. Great multitudes came together to hear and to be healed by him of their infirmities. But he withdrew himself into the desert and prayed. **Luke 5:15,16**

Jesus went out to the mountain to pray and he continued all night in prayer to God. When it was day he called his disciples and chose twelve. **Luke 6:12,13**

At that time Jesus answered, "thank you Father that you hid these things from those who are wise and understanding but revealed them to the people." The Father was pleased. "All things have been delivered to me by my Father. No one knows the Son except the Father, neither does anyone know the Father except the Son and he to whom the Son desires to reveal to him." **Matthew 11:25-27**

Jesus said, "Have the people sit down." Now there was much grass in that place. So the people sat down in number about five thousand men. Jesus took the loaves and having "given thanks," he told the disciples "give out the loaves and fish and let them have as much as they want." When they were filled he said to his disciples, "Gather up
the broken pieces which are left over and nothing would be lost." So they gathered them up and filled twelve baskets with broken pieces from the five barley loaves which were left over by those who had eaten.

When the people saw the sign which Jesus did they said, "This is truly the prophet who comes into the world." Jesus perceiving that they
were about to come and take him by force to make him king. Jesus withdrew again to the mountain by himself.
John 6:10-15, Matthew 14:19, Mark 6:41, Luke 9:16

After he had sent the multitudes away Jesus went up into the mountain by himself to pray. **Matthew 14:23, Mark 6:46, John 6:15**

As he was praying the disciples came upon him and Jesus asked them, "Who do the multitudes say that I am?"

They answered, "'John the Baptizer,' but others say, 'Elijah' and others that one of the old prophets has risen again."

He said to them, "But who do you say that I am?"

Peter answered, "The Christ of God." **Luke 9:18-20**

About eight days later he took with him Peter, James, John and went up onto the mountain to pray. As he was praying, the appearance of his face was altered, and his clothing became white and dazzling. Two men were talking with him who were Moses and Elijah who appeared in glory and spoke of his departure which he was about to accomplish at Jerusalem. **Luke 9:28-36**

When Jesus finished praying in a certain place, one of his disciples said to him, "Lord teach us to pray, just as John taught his disciples."

He said to them, "When you pray, say,

'Our Father in heaven,
may your name be kept holy.

May your Kingdom come.
May your will be done on earth, as it is in heaven.

Give us day by day our daily bread.
Forgive us our sins,
for we ourselves also forgive everyone who is indebted to us.
Bring us not into temptation,
but deliver us from the evil one.'" **Luke 11:1-4**

Jesus said, "Take away the stone."

Martha, the sister of Lazarus, who was dead said to him, "Lord, by this time there is a stench, for he has been dead four days."

Jesus said to her, "Didn't I tell you that if you believed, you would see God's glory?" So they took away the stone from the place where Lazarus was lying.

Jesus lifted up his eyes and said, "Father thank you that you listened to me. I know that you always listen to me." But because of the people standing around Jesus said this. So that they may believe that you sent me."

When he had said this, he cried with a loud voice, "Lazarus, come out!"

Lazarus came out bound hand and foot with wrappings and his face was wrapped with a cloth.

Jesus said to them, "Free him, and let him go." **John 11:39-44**

When you pray good things happen.

REWARDS - Jesus said, "He who receives you receives me, and he who receives me receives him who sent me. He who receives a prophet in the name of a prophet will receive a prophet's reward. He who receives a righteous man in the name of a righteous man will receive a righteous man's reward. Whoever gives one of these little ones just a cup of cold water to drink will in no way will he lose his reward." **Matthew 10:40-42**

Jesus said to his disciples, "If anyone desires to come after me let him deny himself, take up his cross and follow me. For whoever desires to save his life will lose it and whoever will lose his life for my sake will find it. For what will it profit a man if he gains the whole world and forfeits his soul? What will a man give in exchange for his soul? For the Son of Man will come in glory of his Father with his angels and then he will render to everyone according to his deeds. Most certainly I tell you, there are some standing here who will in no way taste of death until they see the Son of Man coming in his Kingdom." **Matthew 16:24-28**

Jesus said, "I tell you, that two of you will agree on anything and ask for it, it will be done for them by my Father who is in heaven. For where two or three are gathered together in my name, there I am in the middle of them." **Matthew 18:19,20**

When a great multitude come together and people from every city would come to see him, he would speak in parables.

Jesus said, "The farmer went out to sow his seed. As he sowed, some fell along the road and it was trampled under foot and the birds of the sky devoured it. Other seed fell on the rock and as soon as it grew, it withered away, because it had no moisture. Other fell amid the thorns and the thorns grew and choked it. Other fell on the good ground and grew, produced one hundred times as much fruit." As he said these things, he called out, "He who has ears to hear, let him hear!" **Luke 8:4-8**

Jesus said, "But when you are invited, go and sit in the lowest place, so that when he who invited you to come and may tell

you, 'Friend, move up higher.' Then you will be honored in the presence of all who sit at the table with you. For everyone who exalts himself will be humbled and whoever humbles himself will be exalted." **Luke 14:10,11**

Jesus answered them, "My teaching is not mine, but the one who sent me. If anyone desires to do God's will and he will know God's will whether it is from God or from me. He who speaks about himself seeks his own glory but the one who seeks the glory of the one who sent him is true." **John 7:16-18**

Jesus said, "But he who is greatest among you will be your servant. Whoever exalts himself will be humbled, and whoever humbles himself will be exalted." **Matthew 23:11,12**

JUSTICE - Jesus spoke this parable to certain people who were convinced of their own righteousness and who despised all others.

"Two men went up into the temple to pray, one was a Pharisee and the other was a tax collector.

The Pharisee stood and prayed to himself. God thank you, that I am not like the rest of men, extortionists, unrighteous, adulterers, or even like this tax collector. I fast twice a week. I give tithes to all that I get.

But the tax collector standing far away, wouldn't even lift up his eyes to heaven but beat his breast saying, God be merciful to me a sinner. The man went down to his house justified. Anyone who

exalts himself will be humbled and anyone who humbles himself will be exalted." **Luke 18:9-14**

Jesus said, "Most certainly, he who hears my word and believes him who sent me has eternal life and doesn't come into judgment but passed out of death into life.

When the dead hears the Son of God's voice, they will live. For as the Father has life in himself also the Son has life in himself and has authority to execute judgment because he is the son of man. Don't marvel at this, for the hour comes in which all who are in the tombs will hear his voice and they will come out and those who have done good will be resurrected to life and those who have done evil will go to the resurrection of judgment. I will judge and my judgment is righteous because I don't seek my own will but the will of my Father who sent me." **John 5:24-30**

Jesus said, "Don't judge and you won't be judged. Don't condemn and you won't be condemned. Set free and you will be set free. Give and it will be given to you. For with the same measure you measure it will be measured back to you."
Luke 6:37,38

THOSE THAT PREACH "FAITH ALONE "
The Protestant belief, specifically among Evangelicals or Born Again Christians, known as 'faith alone' refers to the receiving of salvation through faith alone. This belief goes beyond just faith and also includes the evidence of salvation through love and hope. (Taken from on line)

FAITH ONLY RELIGION - Don't bet your salvation on what someone said, that's not in the bible and ignore what Jesus Christ, who is God, said about the Eucharist that's in the bible." God didn't say anything about "faith alone." Suggest, that you get serious about your religion. Hell is a terrible place to be especially when you are in that place forever.

**Jesus answered them, "Isn't this because you are mistaken, not knowing the Scriptures, nor the power of God?"
Mark 12:24**

Jesus said, "that Hell is a place where you are cast into the the fire of Hell where the fire will never be quenched and where your body will not die." Mark 9:47,48

Jesus said, "Don't be afraid of those who kill the body and are not able to kill the soul. Rather fear the one who is able to destroy both the body and the soul." Matthew 10:28

Jesus said, "He that is not with me is against me. He who doesn't gather with me scatters." Luke 11:23

Jesus said, "Anyone who confesses me before men, I will confess him before my Father who is in heaven. But whoever denies me before men, I will deny him before my Father who is in heaven." Matthew 10:32,33

They said to Jesus, "What must we do, that we may work the works of God?"
Jesus answered them,"This is the works of God, that you believe me whom God has sent." John 6:28,29

For God so loved the world that he gave his only Son. Whoever believes in him will not perish and have eternal life.
For God didn't send his Son into the world to judge the world but that the world should be saved through him.
John 3:16,17

Jesus said,"The Son of Man goes even as it is written of him but woe to that man whom the Son of Man is betrayed! It would be better for that man wasn't born."

Matthew 26:20-24

They said, "Lord when did we see you hungry, thirsty, a stranger, naked, sick or in prison and we didn't help you?"

Jesus answered them. Most certainly I tell you, when you didn't do it to one of the least of these, you didn't do it to me. Those will go away into eternal punishment and the righteous into eternal life." Matthew 25:44-46

Jesus said, "Woe to you who are rich! For you have received your reward. Woe to you who are full now, for you will be hungry. Woe to you who laugh now, for you will mourn and weep. Woe when men speak well of you, for their fathers did the same thing to the false prophets." **Luke 6:24-26**

Jesus said, "I tell you, love your enemies, do good to those who hate you, bless those who curse you and pray for those who mistreat you. Those who strikes you on the cheek, offer the other cheek. Those who takes away your cloak, don't withhold your coat to others. Give to everyone who asks for your goods. Those who takes your goods, don't asked for them back."

Jesus said, "As you would like people to do to you, do exactly to them. If you love those who love you, what credit is that to you? For even sinners love those who love them. If you do good to those who do good to you, what credit is that to you? For even sinners do the same. If you lend to those from whom you hope to receive, what credit is that to you? Even sinners lend to sinners, to receive back as much. But love your enemies and do good expect nothing back your reward will be great and you will be children of the Most High. Be merciful as your Father is merciful." **Luke 6:27-36**

Jesus said, "Don't judge and you won't be judged. Don't condemn and you won't be condemned. Set free and you will be set free. Give and it will be given to you. For with the same measure you measure it will be measured back to you."
Luke 6:37,38

Jesus said, "Someone who has bathed only needs to have his feet washed and you will be clean but not all of you." For he knew him who would betray him therefore he said, "You are not all clean."

So when he had finish washing their feet and put his outer garment back on He sat down and he said "Do you know what I have

done for you? You call me, 'Teacher' and 'Lord.' You are correct, so I am. I have washed your feet. Now you wash one another feet. For I have given you an example that you should do as I have done for you. Most certainly I tell you a servant is not greater than his lord, neither is one who is sent greater than
he who sent him. If you know these things and do them and blessed are you, for doing them." **John 13:10-17**

Jesus said, "Be careful that you don't do your charitable givings in public or else you have no reward from your Father who is in heaven. Therefore, don't brag to others about your merciful deeds like the hypocrites do so that they may get glory from others. Most certainly I tell you, they have received their reward. But when you do merciful deeds, don't let your left hand know what your right hand is doing so that your merciful deeds may be in secret and your Father who sees you in secret will reward you." **Matthew 6:1-4**

THOSE THAT PREACH "RAPTURE"

Paul's letter to the Thessalonians:
Finally brothers, we beg and exhort you in the Lord Jesus, that as you received from us how you ought to walk and to please God, that you abound more and more. For you know what instructions we gave you through the Lord Jesus. For this is the will of God: your sanctification, that you abstain from sexual immorality, that each one of you know how to control his own body in sanctification and honor, not in the passion of lust, even as the Gentiles who don't know God, that no one should take advantage of and wrong a brother or sister in this matter; because the Lord is an avenger in all these things, as also we forewarned you and testified. For God called us not for uncleanness, but in sanctification. Therefore he who rejects this doesn't reject man, but God, who has also given his Holy Spirit to you.
Finally then, brothers, we beg and exhort you in the Lord Jesus, that as you received from us how you ought to walk and to please God, that you abound more and more. For you know

what instructions we gave you through the Lord Jesus. For this is

the will of God: your sanctification, that you abstain from sexual immorality, that each one of you know how to control his own body in sanctification and honor, not in the passion of lust, even as the Gentiles who don't know God, that no one should take advantage of and wrong a brother or sister in this matter; because the Lord is an avenger in all these things, as also we forewarned you and testified. For God called us not for

uncleanness, but in sanctification. Therefore he who rejects this

doesn't reject man, but God, who has also given his Holy Spirit to you.

But concerning brotherly love, you have no need that one write to you. For you yourselves are taught by God to love one another, for indeed you do it toward all the brothers who are in all Macedonia. But we exhort you, brothers, that you abound more and more and that you make it your ambition to lead a quiet life and to do your own business, and to work with your own hands, even as we instructed you that you may walk properly toward those who are outside, and may have need of nothing.

But we don't want you to be ignorant, brothers, concerning those who have fallen asleep, so that you don't grieve like the rest, who have no hope. For if we believe that Jesus died and rose again, even so God will bring with him those who have fallen asleep in Jesus. For this we tell you by the word of the Lord, that we who are alive, who are left until the coming of the
Lord, will in no way precede those who have fallen asleep. For the Lord himself will descend from heaven with a shout, with the voice of the archangel and with God's trumpet. The dead in Christ will rise first then we who are alive, who are left, will be caught up together with them in the clouds, to meet the Lord in
the air. So we will be with the Lord forever. Therefore comfort one another with these words. Paul's letter 1 Thessalonians 4:15-17 is being call "Rapture."

Paul letter to the Corinthians:

Now I declare to you, brothers, the Good News which I preached to you, which also you received, in which you also stand, by

which also you are saved, if you hold firmly the word which I preached to you unless you believed in vain. For I delivered to you first of all that which I also received that Christ died for our sins according to the Scriptures that he was buried that he was raised on the third day according to the Scriptures and that he appeared to Cephas, then to the twelve. Then he appeared to over five hundred brothers at once, most of whom remain until now, but some have also fallen asleep. He appeared to James, then to all the apostles and last of all, as to the child born at the wrong time, he appeared to me. For I am the least of the apostles, who is not worthy to be called an apostle, because I persecuted the assembly of God. But by the grace of God I am what I am. His grace which was given to me was not futile but I worked more than all of them, yet not I, but the grace of God which was with me. Whether then it is I or they, so we preach, and so you believed.

Now if Christ is preached, that he has been raised from the dead, how do some among you say that there is no resurrection of the dead? But if there is no resurrection of the dead, neither has Christ been raised. If Christ has not been raised, then our preaching is in vain, and your faith also is in vain. Yes, we have found false witnesses of God, because we testified about God that he raised up Christ, whom he didn't raise up, if it is so that

the dead are not raised. For if the dead aren't raised, neither has Christ been raised. If Christ has not been raised, your faith is vain and you are still have your sins. Who are fallen asleep in Christ have perished. If we have only hoped in Christ in this life, we are of all men most pitiable.

But now Christ has been raised from the dead. He became the first fruit of those who are asleep. For since death came by man, the resurrection of the dead also came by man. For as in Adam all die, so also in Christ all will be made alive. But each in his own order. Christ the first fruits, then those who are Christ's, at his coming. Then the end comes, when he will deliver up the Kingdom to God, even the Father, when he will have abolished all rule and all authority and power. For he must reign until he has put all his enemies under his feet. The last enemy that will be abolished is death. "He put all things in subjection under his feet." But when he says, "All things are put in subjection", it is evident that he is excepted who subjected all things to him. When all things have been subjected to him, then the Son will also himself be subjected to him who subjected all things to him, that God may be all in all.

Or else what will they do who are baptized for the dead? If the dead aren't raised at all, why then are they baptized for the dead? Why do we also stand in jeopardy every hour? I affirm, by the boasting in you which I have in Christ Jesus our Lord, I die daily. If I fought with animals at Ephesus for human purposes, what does it profit me? If the dead are not raised, then "let's eat and drink, for tomorrow we die. " Don't be deceived! "Evil companionship's corrupt good morals." Wake up righteously, and don't sin, for some have no knowledge of God. I say this to your shame.

But someone will say, "How are the dead raised?" and, "With what kind of body do they come?" You foolish one, that which you yourself sow is not made alive unless it dies. That which you sow, you don't sow the body that will be, but a bare grain, maybe of wheat, or of some other kind. But God gives it a body even as it pleased him, and to each seed a body of its own. All flesh is not the same flesh, but there is one flesh of men, another flesh of animals, another of fish, and another of birds. There are

also celestial bodies and terrestrial bodies but the glory of the celestial differs from that of the terrestrial. There is one glory of the sun, another glory of the moon, and another glory of the stars for one star differs from another star in glory. So also is the resurrection of the dead. The body is sown perishable it is raised imperishable. It is sown in dishonor it is raised in glory. It is sown in weakness, it is raised in power. It is sown a natural body it is raised a spiritual body. There is a natural body and there is also a spiritual body.

So also it is written, "The first man, Adam, became a living soul." The last Adam became a life-giving spirit. However that which is spiritual isn't first, but that which is natural, then that which is spiritual. The first man is of the earth, made of dust. The second man is the Lord from heaven. As is the one made of dust, such are those who are also made of dust; and as is the heavenly, such are they also that are heavenly.

As we have borne the image of those made of dust, let's also bear the image of the heavenly. C. We will not all sleep, but we will all be changed, in a moment, in the twinkling of an eye, at the last trumpet. For the trumpet will sound and the dead will be raised incorruptible, and we will be changed. For this perishable body must become imperishable, and this mortal must put on immortality. But when this perishable body will have become imperishable, and this mortal will have put on immortality, then what is written will happen: "Death is swallowed up in victory."

"Death where is your sting? Hades, where is your victory?"

The sting of death is sin and the power of sin is the law. But thanks be to God, who gives us the victory through our Lord Jesus Christ. Therefore, my beloved brothers, be steadfast, immovable, always abounding in the Lord's work, because you know that your labor is not in vain in the Lord.
1 Corinthians 15:1-58

FACTS ABOUT THE WORD "RAPTURE"

The word "RAPTURE" is not in the bible. The meaning of the word rapture is to carry off or to catch up. Certain churches didn't know what Paul was talking about. In 1830 they came up with the word rapture and started preaching "Rapture." But they didn't mention the letter to Corinthians that corrected the letter to the Thessalonians and they did not mention God's statement in Genesis.

Jesus answered them, "Isn't this because you are mistaken, not knowing the Scriptures, nor the power of God?"
Mark 12:24

Jesus said, "He that is not with me is against me. He who doesn't gather with me scatters." Luke 11:23

Jesus said, "The Son of Man goes even as it is written of him but woe to that man whom the Son of Man is betrayed! It would be better for that man if he wasn't born."

Matthew 26:20-24

Jesus said, "that Hell is a place where you are cast into the the fire of Hell where the fire will never be quenched and where their bodies will not die." Mark 9:43-48

Suggest, that you get serious about your religion. Hell is terrible place to be and especially forever.

Jesus said, "Don't be afraid of those who kill the body and are not able to kill the soul. Rather fear the one who is able to destroy both the body and the soul." Matthew 10:28

Paul wrote these words in a letter to the Thessalonians:

So "we" will be with the The dead in Christ will rise first, then we who are alive, who are left, will be caught up together with them in the clouds, to meet the Lord in the air. Lord forever. Therefore comfort one another with these words. **1 Thessalonians 4:1-18**

Paul wrote these words in a letter to the Corinthians: Now I say this, brothers, that flesh and blood can't inherit God's Kingdom; neither does the perishable inherit imperishable.
1 Corinthians 15:1-54

In the book of Genesis God said, "You will eat bread by the sweat of your face until you return to the ground, for you were taken out of it. For you are dust, and you shall return to dust." **Genesis 3:1**

Jesus answered them, "This is the work of God, that you believe me whom God has sent." John 6:28,29

The Thessalonians Community believed that they will be taken up into Heaven.

In 1830 certain churches didn't mention 1Corinthians 15:1-54 that corrects the 1Thessalonians 4:15-17 statement and 1Thessalonians 4:15-17 contradicts what God is saying in Genesis 3:1 **Jesus therefore said to those Jews who had believed him, "If you remain in my word then you are truly my disciples. You will know the truth and the truth will set you free."**
John 8:31,32

Based on these facts I believe that the bible is correct that Paul wrote both letters to two different communities. But I don't believe the words of Paul. I think that he got confused when he wrote the letter to the Thessalonians.

I don't know the subject matter that Paul was talking about but nothing has happen for almost two thousand years.

I don't believe that what Paul is describing in 1Thesssalonians 4:15-17 will happen to us. Don't bet your eternity on it. It's not going to happen.

Jesus said, "You search the Scriptures, because you think that in them you have eternal life. Yet you will not come to me, that you may have life. I don't receive glory from men. But I know you, that you don't have God's love in yourselves. I have come in my Father's name, and you don't receive me. If another comes in his own name, you will receive him. How can you believe, who receive glory from one another and you don't seek the glory that only comes from God?" **John 5:39-44**

Jesus said, "I Don't think that I will send you to the Father. Even Moses would accuse you whom you have set your hope. For if you believed Moses, you would believe me, for he wrote about me. But if you don't believe his writings, how will you believe my words?"-**John 5:45-47**

THOSE THAT MISLEAD YOU
Jesus said, "Be careful that no one leads you astray. For many will come in my name, saying, 'I am he!' and will lead many astray." **Mark 13:5,6**

Jesus said, "If anyone tells you, 'Look, here is the Christ!' or, 'Look, there!' don't believe it. For there will arise false christs and false prophets and will show signs and wonders, that they may lead you astray, even the chosen ones. But keep watch." **Mark 13:21-23**

Jesus answered them, "Isn't this because you are mistaken, not knowing the Scriptures, nor the power of God?" **Mark 12:24**

Jesus said to the multitudes, "When you see a cloud rising from the west, immediately you say, 'A shower is coming,' and so it happens. When a south wind blows you say, 'There will be a scorching heat,' and it happens. You hypocrites! You know how to interpret the appearance of the earth and the sky but how is it that you don't interpret God correctly?" **Luke 12:54-56**

Jesus answered them, "Be careful that no one leads you astray. For many will come in my name, saying, I am the Christ, and they will lead many astray." **Matthew 24:4,5**

Jesus said, "Beware of false prophets, who come to you in sheep's clothing, but inwardly are ravening wolves. By their fruits you will know them. Do you gather grapes from thorns or figs from thistles?
Every good tree produces good fruit, but the corrupt tree produces evil fruit. A good tree can't produce evil fruit, neither can a corrupt tree produce good fruit. Every tree that doesn't grow good fruit is cut down and thrown into the fire. By their fruits you will know them."   **Matthew 7:15-20**

Jesus said, "Watch yourselves, for they will deliver you up to councils. You will be beaten in synagogues. You will stand before rulers and kings for my sake, for a testimony to them.

When they lead you away and deliver you up, don't be anxious beforehand, or premeditate what you will say but say whatever will be given you in that hour. For it is not you who speak but the Holy Spirit.

Jesus added, Brother will deliver up brother to death and the father's child. Children will rise up against parents and cause them to be put to death. You will be hated by all men for my name's sake but he who endures to the end will be saved."
Mark 13:9-13

Jesus said, "They will persecute you and will say falsely things against you because of me. Rejoice and be exceedingly glad, for great is your reward in heaven. For that is how they persecuted the prophets who lived before you. **Matthew 5:11,12**

Jesus said, "they will deliver you up to oppression and will kill you. You will be hated by all of the nations for my name's sake. Many will stumble and will deliver up one another and will hate one another. Many false prophets will arise and will lead many astray. Because wickedness will be multiplied, the love of many will grow cold. But he who endures to the end will be saved. This Good News of the Kingdom will be preached in the whole world for a testimony to all the nations and then the end will come." **Matthew 24:9-14**

Jesus said, "If you love me, keep my commandments." **John 14:15**

AN EYE FOR AN EYE - Jesus said, "You have heard that it was said, 'An eye for an eye, and a tooth for a tooth.' But I tell you, don't resist him who is evil but whoever strikes you on your right cheek, also turn to him the other. If anyone sues you to take away your coat, let him have your cloak too. Whoever compels you to go one mile, go two miles. Don't turn away a person who desires to borrow from you." **Matthew 5:38-42**

Jesus said, "Don't judge, so that you won't be judged. For with whatever judgment you judge, you will be judged and with whatever measure you measure, it will be measured to you." **Matthew 7:1,2**

Jesus said "Why do you see the speck that is in your brother's eye, but don't consider the beam that is in your own eye? How can you tell your brother, 'Let me remove the speck from your eye,' and there the beam is in your own eye? You hypocrite! First remove the beam out of your own eye and then you can see clearly to remove the speck out of your brother's eye." **Matthew 7:3-5**

SCANDALS -Jesus said, "Woe to the world because of occasions of stumbling! For it must be that the occasions come, but woe to that person through whom the occasion comes! If your hand or your foot causes you to stumble, cut it off and cast it from you. It is better for you to enter into life maimed or crippled, rather than having two hands or two feet to be cast into the eternal fire. If your eye causes you to stumble, pluck it out and cast it from you. It is better for you to enter into life with one eye, rather than having two eyes to be cast into the Hell of fire. See that you don't despise one of these little ones, for I tell you that in heaven their angels always see the face of my Father who is in heaven.

For the Son of Man came to save that which was lost."

Matthew 18:7-11

JESUS RECORDED MIRACLES

The Wedding Feast of Cana

The third day, there was a wedding in Cana of Galilee. Jesus' mother was there. Jesus also was invited, with his disciples, to the wedding. When the wine ran out, Jesus' mother said to him, "They have no wine."

Jesus said to her, "Woman, what does that have to do with us? My hour has not yet come."

His mother said to the servants, "Whatever he says to you do it." Now there were six water pots of stone set there after the Jews' way of purifying, containing two or three metretes apiece.

Jesus said to them, "Fill the water pots with water." So they filled them up to the brim. He said to them, "Now draw some out and take it to the head of the feast."

So they did. When the head of the feast tasted the water now become wine and didn't know where it came from but the servants who had drawn the water knew.

The head of the feast called the bridegroom and said to him, "Everyone serves the good wine first and when the guests have drunk freely then they serve the wine that is not as good. You have kept the good wine until now!"

This beginning of his signs Jesus did in Cana of Galilee, and revealed his glory and his disciples believed in him. **John 2:1-11**

Jesus Heals an Official's son
After the two days he went out from there and went into Galilee. For Jesus himself testified that a prophet has no honor in his own country. So when he came into Galilee, the Galileans received him, having seen all the things that he did in Jerusalem at the feast, for they also went to the feast Jesus came therefore again to Cana of Galilee, where he made the water into wine. There was a certain nobleman whose son was sick at Capernaum. When he heard that Jesus had come out of Judea into Galilee, he went to him and begged him that he would come down and heal his son for he was at the point of death.
Jesus said to him, "Unless you see signs and wonders, you   don't believe."

The nobleman said to him, "Sir, come down before my child dies."

Jesus said to him, "Go your way. Your son lives."

The man believed the word that Jesus spoke to him and he went his way. As he was now going down, his servants met him and reported, saying "Your child lives!" So he inquired of them the hour when he began to get better.

They said to him, "Yesterday at the seventh hour, the fever left him." So the father knew that it was at that hour in which Jesus said to him, "Your son lives." He believed, as did his whole house. This is again the second sign that Jesus did having come out of Judea into Galilee. **John 4:43-54**

Jesus Drives Out an Evil Spirit

They went into Capernaum and immediately on the Sabbath day he entered into the synagogue and taught. They were astonished at his teaching, for he taught them as having authority and not as the scribes. Immediately there was in their synagogue a man with an unclean spirit and he cried out, saying, "Ha! What do we have to do with you Jesus, you Nazarene? Have you come to destroy us? I know you who you are, the Holy One of God!"

Jesus rebuked him saying, "Be quiet and come out of him!"
The unclean spirit convulsing him and crying with a loud voice and he came out of him.
They were all amazed, so that they questioned among themselves saying, "What is this? A new teaching? For with authority he commands even the unclean spirits and they obey him!" **Mark 1:21-27, Luke 4:31-36**

Jesus Heals Peter's Mother-in-Law
When they came out of the synagogue they went into the house of Simon and Andrew with James and John. Now Simon's wife's mother lay sick with a fever and immediately they told Jesus about her. He came and took her by the hand and raised her up. The fever left her immediately and she served them.
Mark 1:29-31, Matthew 8:14,15, Luke 4:38,39

Jesus Heals Many Sick
At evening when the sun had set they brought to him all who were sick and those who were possessed by demons. All the city was gathered together at the door. He healed many who were sick with various diseases and cast out many demons. He didn't allow the demons to speak because they knew him.
Mark 1:32-34, Matthew 8:16,17, Luke 4:40,41

First Miraculous Catch of Fish
Jesus was by the lake of Gennesaret when he saw two fishing boats and the fishermen were washing their nets.

He entered into Simon's boat and Jesus asked him, "To put out a little from the land." He sat down and taught the multitudes from the boat. When he had finished speaking he said to Simon, "Put out into the deep and let down your net for a catch."

Simon answered him, "Master we worked all night and took nothing but at your word I will let down the net." When they had done this they caught a great multitude of fish and their net was breaking. They beckoned to their partners in the other boat to come and help them. They came and filled both boats and they began to sink.

When they arrive at the shore Simon fell down at Jesus' knees saying,
"Lord depart from me for I am a sinful man." Simon was amazed of the large number of fish which they had caught. So were James and John, sons of Zebedee, who were partners with Simon. They left everything and followed Jesus.

Jesus said to Simon, "Don't be afraid. From now on you will be catching people." **Luke 5:1-11**

Jesus Cleanses a Man with Leprosy
When Jesus came down from the mountain, great multitudes followed him. A leper came to him and saying, "Lord, make me clean."

Jesus stretched out his hand and touched him saying, "I want you to be made clean." Immediately his leprosy left him. Jesus said to him, "See that you tell nobody but go show yourself to the priest and offer the gift that Moses commanded as a testimony to them." **Matthew 1-4, Mark 1:40-45, Luke 5:12-14**

Jesus Heals a Paralyzed Servant
When he came into Capernaum, a centurion came to him asking him for help saying, "Lord my servant lies in the house paralyzed and grievously tormented."

Jesus said, "I will come and heal him."

The centurion answered, "Lord I'm not worthy for you to come under my roof. Just say the word and my servant will be healed. For I am also a man with authority and having under myself soldiers. I tell this one, 'Go,' and he goes and tell another, 'Come,' and he comes and tell my servant, 'Do this,' and he does it."
When Jesus heard it, he marveled and said, to those who followed, "Most certainly I tell you, not even in Israel have I found an individual with such great faith.

I tell you that many will come from the east and the west and will sit down with Abraham, Isaac, and Jacob in the Kingdom of Heaven, but the children of their Kingdom will be thrown out into the outer darkness where there will be weeping and gnashing of teeth."

Jesus said to the centurion, "Go your way. Let it be done for you as you have believed." His servant was healed at that hour. **Matthew 8:5-13, Luke 7:1-10**

Jesus Heals a Paralytic
He entered into a boat and crossed over and came into his own city. They brought to him a man who was paralyzed lying on a bed. Jesus seeing their faith said to the paralytic, "Son cheer up! Your sins are forgiven you." Some of the scribes said to themselves, "This man blasphemes."

Jesus, knowing their thoughts said, "Why do you think evil in your hearts? For which is easier, to say, 'Your sins are forgiven' or to say, 'Get up, and walk?' But that you may know that the Son of Man has authority on earth to forgive sins" he said to the paralytic "Get up and take up your mat and go home." He arose and departed to his house.

But when the multitudes saw it they marveled and glorified God, who had given such authority to me.
Matthew 9:1-8, Mark 2:1-12, Luke 5:17-26

Jesus Heals a Man's Withered Hand

He departed from there and went into their synagogue. And there was a man with a withered hand. They asked him, "Is it lawful to heal on the Sabbath day?"

Jesus said to them, "What man is there among you who has one sheep and if this one falls into a pit on the Sabbath day wouldn't he grab on to it and lift it out? Of how much more value then is a man than a sheep! It is lawful to do good on the Sabbath day." Then he told the man, "Stretch out your hand." He stretched it out and the hand was restored just like the other. But the Pharisees went out and conspired against him and how they might destroy him. **Matthew 12:9-14, Mark 3:1-6, Luke 6:6-11**

Jesus Raises a Widow's Son From the Dead

Jesus went to a city called Nain. Many of his disciples with a great multitude went with him. When Jesus came near the gate of the city there was a crowd carrying out the only son of a widow. When the Lord saw her, he had compassion for her and said to her, "Don't cry." Jesus came near and touched the coffin and the bearers stood still.

Jesus said, "Young man, arise!" He who was dead sat up and began to speak. Jesus gave him to his mother.

Fear took hold of all and they glorified God saying, "A great prophet has arisen among us!" This report went out concerning him in the whole of Judea and in all the surrounding region. **Luke 7:11-17**

Jesus Calms a Storm on the Sea

When he got into a boat, his disciples followed him. Jesus was asleep when a violent storm came up on the horizon and the waves started covering the boat.

The disciples woke up Jesus saying, "Save us, Lord! We are sinking!"

Jesus said to them, "Why are you fearful O you of little faith?" Jesus got up rebuked the wind and the sea and there was a great calm.

The men marveled saying, "What kind of man is this, that even the wind and the sea obey him?"
Matthew 8:23-27, Mark 4:35-41, Luke 8:22-25

Jesus Casts Demons into a Herd of Pigs
When Jesus arrived on the other side of the country of Gergesenes. Two people came out of tombs and met him. They
were possessed and the demons were exceedingly vicious so that nobody could pass their way. They cried out saying, "What
do you want from us Jesus, Son of God? Have you come here to torment us before our time?" Now there was a herd of pigs feeding far away from them. The demons begged him saying "If you cast us out permit us to go away into the herd of pigs."

Jesus said to them, "Go!"

They came out and went into the herd of pigs and the whole herd of pigs rushed down the cliff into the sea and died in the water. Those who fed them fled and went away into the city and told everything that happened including those who were possessed with demons. **Matthew 8:28-33,Mark 5:1-20,**
Luke 8:26-39

Jesus Heals a Woman
A woman who had a discharge of blood for twelve years came behind him and touched the fringe of his garment for she

said within herself "If I just touch his garment, I will be cured."

But Jesus, turning around and seeing her said, "Daughter cheer up! Your faith has saved you." And the woman was cured from that hour. **Matthew 9:20-22, Mark25-34, Luke 8:42-48**

Jesus Raises Jairus' Daughter

When Jesus came into the ruler's house and saw the flute players and the crowd in noisy disorder he said to them, "Make room because the girl isn't dead but sleeping."

They begin to ridicule him. When the crowd was sent out he entered in took her by the hand and the girl arose. The report of this went out into all the land. **Matthew 9:23-26, Mark 5:35-43, Luke 8:49-56**

Jesus Heals Two Blind Men

As Jesus passed by two blind men followed him and called out saying, "Have mercy on us, son of David!" When he had come into the house the blind men follow him.

Jesus said to them, "Do you believe that I am able to do this?" They told him "Yes Lord."

Then he touched their eyes saying, "Because of your faith let it be done." Then their eyes opened. Jesus strictly commanded them saying, "See that no one knows about this." But they went out and spread his fame in all the land.
Matthew 9:27-31

Jesus Heals a Man

As they went out a mute man who was possessed by a demon was brought to him. When the demon was cast out the mute man started speaking. The multitudes marveled saying, "Nothing like this has ever been seen in Israel!"

But the Pharisees said, "By the prince of the demons, he casts out demons." **Matthew 9:32-34**

Jesus Heals an invalid

There was a feast and Jesus went up to Jerusalem. Now in Jerusalem by the sheep gate, there is a pool, which is called in Hebrew, "Bethesda", having five porches.

In those days laid a great multitude of those who were sick, blind, lame, or paralyzed, waiting for the moving of the water for an angel went down at certain times into the pool and stirred up the water. Whoever stepped in first after the stirring of the water was healed of whatever disease he had. A certain man was there who had been sick for thirty-eight years.

When Jesus saw him lying there and knew that he had been sick for a long time he asked him, "Do you want to be made well?"
The sick man answered him, "Sir, I have no one to put me into the pool when the water is stirred up but while I'm coming, another steps down before me."

Jesus said to him, "Arise take up your mat and walk."
Immediately the man was made well and took up his mat and walked.

Now on the day of the Sabbath. The Jews said to him who was cured, "It is the Sabbath. It is not lawful for you to carry the mat."

He answered them, "He who made me well said to me, 'Take up your mat and walk.'"

Then they asked him, "Who is the man who told you, 'Take up your mat and walk'?"

But he who was healed didn't know who he was for Jesus had withdrawn from the crowd.

Afterward Jesus found him in the temple and said to him, "Behold you are made well. Sin no more so that nothing worse happens to you."

The man went away and told the Jews that it was Jesus who had made him well. **John:1-15**

Jesus Feeds 5,000 Plus Women and Children

Now when Jesus heard this he withdrew from there in a boat to a deserted place. When the multitudes heard it, they followed him on foot from the cities. Jesus went out and he saw a great multitude. He had compassion on them and healed their sick. When evening had come his disciples came to him saying, "This place is deserted and the hour is already late. Send the multitudes away that they may go into the villages, and buy themselves food."

But Jesus said to them, "They don't need to go away. You give them something to eat.

"They told him, "We only have here five loaves and two fish."

Jesus said, "Bring the loves and fish her to me." He commanded the multitudes to sit down on the grass and he took the five loaves and the two fish and looking up to heaven he blessed, broke and gave the loaves to the disciples and the disciples gave to the multitudes. They all ate and were filled. They took up twelve baskets full of that which remained left over from the broken pieces. Those who ate were about five thousand men in addition to women and children. **Matthew 14:13-21,**
Mark 6:30-44, Luke 9:10-17, John 6:1-15

Jesus Walks on Water

Jesus told the disciples, "to get into the boat and go ahead of him to the other side while he sent the multitudes away." After the multitudes left he went up into the mountain by himself to pray.

When evening had come, he was alone. The boat was now in the middle of the sea distressed by the waves for the wind was increasing.
In the fourth watch of the night Jesus came to them walking on the water. When the disciples saw him walking on the water, they

were troubled saying, "It's a ghost!" and in fear they cried out.
But immediately Jesus spoke to them, saying, "It is I! Don't be afraid."

Peter answered him and said, "Lord, if it is you command me to come to you on the waters."

He said, "Come!"

Peter stepped down from the boat and walked on the waters to Jesus. But when he saw that the wind was strong, he was afraid and begin to sink, he cried out saying, "Lord, save me!"

Immediately Jesus stretched out his hand took hold of him and said to him, "You of little faith, why did you doubt?" When they got up into the boat the wind ceased.

Those who were in the boat came and worshiped him saying, "You are truly the Son of God!" **Matthew 14:22-33, Mark 6:45-52, John 6:16-21**

Jesus Heals Many Sick
When they had crossed over they came to the land of Gennesaret. The people recognized him. The people traveled to all the surrounding region and brought back the sick to him. They begged him that they might just touch the fringe of his garment. They knew that many people were cured because they touched the fringe of his garment. **Matthew 14:34-36, Mark 6:53-56**

Jesus Heals a Gentile Woman

Jesus went out from there and withdrew into the region of Tyre and Sidon.

A Canaanite woman crying came out from those borders saying, "Have mercy on me, son of David! My daughter is possessed by a demon!" Jesus did not answered.

His disciples came and ask him to send her away for she keeps following us. Jesus answered, "I only was sent to the lost sheep of the house of Israel."

But she came and worshiped him saying, "Lord help me."

he answered, "It is not appropriate to take the children's bread and throw it to the dogs."

She said, "Yes Lord but even the dogs eat the crumbs which fall from their masters' table."

Then Jesus answered her, "Woman great is your faith. Be it done to you even as you desire." Her daughter was healed at that hour. **Matthew 15:21-28, Mark 7:24-30**

Jesus Heals a Man

Jesus departed from the borders of Tyre and Sidon and came to the sea of Galilee through the middle of the region of Decapolis. They brought Him a person who was deaf and had an impediment in his speech. They asked Jesus to lay his hand on him. Privately Jesus took him aside from the multitude and put his fingers into his ears and touched his tongue. Looking up to heave He said to him, "Ephphatha!" that is, "Be opened" Immediately his ears were opened, the impediment of his tongue was released and he spoke clearly. He commanded them that they should tell no one but the more he commanded them the more widely they proclaimed it.

They were astonished beyond measure saying, "He has cured him. He makes even the deaf hear and the mute speak!" **Mark:7:31-37**

Jesus Feeds 4,000

Jesus summoned his disciples and said, "I have compassion on the multitude because they been with me for three days and they have nothing to eat. I don't want to send them away hungry or they might faint on the way."

The disciples said to him, "Where can we get so many loaves in a deserted place for so many people?"

Jesus said to them, "How many loaves do you have?"
They said, "Seven loaves and a few fish."

Jesus told the crowd to sit down then He gave thanks for the loaves and the fish gave them to the disciples. The disciples gave them to the people. They all ate and were filled. They took up seven baskets full of the broken pieces that were left over. The
four thousand men, women and children ate and were satisfied. Then he sent the people away. Then Jesus and the disciples got into the boat and went to the borders of Magdala.
Matthew 15:32-39,Mark 8:-13

Jesus Heals a Blind Man

When He came to Bethsaida. They brought a blind man to him, and asked Jesus to cure him. Jesus took hold of the blind man by his hand and took him out of the village. Then he place spat on his eyes and laid his hands on him, Jesus asked him if he saw anything. He looked up and the man said, "I see men that look like trees walking." Jesus laid his hands on his eyes. He looked intently and his eyes were restored. The man saw everyone clearly. Jesus sent the man away to his house saying, "Don't tell anyone in the village what happened." **Mark 8:22-26**

Jesus Heals another Blind Man

As he passed by he saw a man that was blind from birth. His disciples asked him, "Rabbi, who is the sinner, the man or his parents that he was born blind?"

Jesus answered, "This man didn't sin, nor did his parents. So that the works of God might be revealed in him."

Jesus said, "I am the light of the world and I must do the will of the Father who sent me." When he had said this he spat on the ground made mud with the saliva anointed the blind man's eyes with the mud and said to him, "Go wash in the pool of Siloam." So he went away washed his eyes and came back seeing.

The neighbors knew that he was blind before. They said, "Isn't this the man who sat and begged?" Others were saying, "It is he." Still others were saying, "He looks like him." the man said, "I am

the one who was blind." They asked him, "How were your eyes opened?" He answered, "A man called Jesus made mud, anointed my eyes and said to me, 'Go to the pool of Siloam and wash your eyes.' "So I went away and washed and now I can see." Then they asked him, "Where is this man called Jesus?" He said, "I don't know." **John 9:1-12**

Jesus heals a boy

When they came to the multitude a man came to him kneeling down to him and saying, "Lord, have mercy on my son for he is epileptic and suffers grievously. He falls into the fire and often into the water. So I brought him to your disciples and they couldn't cure him."

Jesus answered, "Faithless and perverse generation! How long will I be with you? How long will I bear with you? Bring him here to me." Jesus rebuked the demon and it went out of him and the boy was cured at that hour.

Then the disciples came to Jesus privately and said, "Why weren't we able to cast out the demon?"

Jesus said, "Because you did not believe. For most certainly I tell you if you have faith as a grain of mustard seed you will tell this mountain 'Move from here to there,' and it will move and nothing will be impossible for you. **Matthew 17:14-20, Mark 9:14-29, Luke 9:37-43**

Temple Tax in a Fish's Mouth
When they arrive at Capernaum, those who collected the didrachma coins came to Peter and said, "Doesn't your teacher

pay the didrachma?" He said, "Yes."

When he came into the house, Jesus anticipated him saying, "What do you think, Peter? From whom do the kings of the earth receive toll or tribute? From their children or from strangers?"

Peter said to him, "From strangers."

Jesus said to him, "Therefore the children are exempt. But lest we cause them to stumble go to the sea cast a hook and take up the first fish that comes up. When you have opened its mouth you will find a stater coin. Take the coin and give it to them for you and me." **Matthew 17:24-27**

Jesus Heals three people
One possessed by a demon, one blind person and one mute person was brought to him. Jesus healed all three people. All the people were amazed. They said, "Can this be the son of David?" **Matthew 12:22,23, Luke 11:14-23**

Jesus Heals a Women
Jesus was teaching in one of the synagogues on the Sabbath day. There was a woman who had a spirit of infirmity for eighteen years.

She was bent over and couldn't straighten herself up. Jesus laid his hands on her and told her that you are freed from your infirmity and immediately she stood up and glorified God.

The ruler of the synagogue, being indignant because Jesus had healed on the Sabbath said to the people, "There are six days in which men ought to work. Therefore come on those days and be healed and not on the Sabbath day!"

Jesus answered him, "You hypocrites! Doesn't each one of you free his ox or his donkey from the stall on the Sabbath and lead them to water? Ought not this woman being a daughter of Abraham whom Satan had bound eighteen long years be freed from this bondage on the Sabbath day?"

As he said these things, all his adversaries were disappointed and all the people rejoiced for all the glorious things that were done by him. **Luke 13:10-17**

Jesus Heals a Man
Jesus went on the Sabbath into the house of one of the rulers of the Pharisees to eat bread and they were watching him.

A man who had dropsy was in front of Jesus and spoke to the lawyers and Pharisees saying, "Is it lawful to heal on the Sabbath?" But they were silent. Jesus healed him and said, "If your son or an ox fell into the well wouldn't you immediately pull them out on a Sabbath day?" Again they couldn't answer him. **Luke 14:1-6**

Jesus Cleanses Ten Lepers
Jesus was passing along the borders of Samara and Galilee on his way to Jerusalem. As he entered into a certain village ten men who were lepers met him. They were saying, "Jesus have mercy on us!"

he said to them, "Go and show yourselves to the priests." they left and were cleansed. When one of them saw that he was healed turned back and glorify God with a loud voice. The Samaritan fell on his face at Jesus' feet and gave him thanks.

Jesus answered, Wasn't there ten, where are the other nine? Then he said to him, " Go your way. Your faith has healed you." **Luke 17:11-19**

Jesus Raises Lazarus

Lazarus from Bethany where Mary and her sister Martha lived. It was that Mary who had anointed Jesus with ointment and wiped his feet with her hair whose brother Lazarus was sick. The sisters sent for Jesus saying, "Lord, Lazarus whom you have great affection for is sick." By the time Jesus heard that Lazarus was sick he said, "This sickness is not to die but for the glory of God that Jesus may be glorified by it." Now Jesus loved Mary, Martha and Lazarus but when he heard that Lazarus was sick he stayed two days in the place where he was. Then Jesus said to the disciples, "Let's go to Judea."

The disciples asked him, "Rabbi, the Jews were just trying to stone you. Are you sure you want to go there?"

Jesus answered, "Aren't there twelve hours of daylight? If a man walks in the day, he doesn't stumble, because he sees the light of this world. But if a man walks in the night, he stumbles because the light isn't in him. Our friend Lazarus has fallen asleep and I am going so that I will awake him up out of his sleep."

The disciples said, "Lord, if he has fallen asleep, he will recover." Now Jesus had spoken of his death, but they thought that he was asleep. So Jesus said to them plainly that Lazarus is dead. It is better that I was not there so that you may believe. Nevertheless let's go to him."

Thomas who was called Didymus said, to his fellow disciples, "Let's go that we may die with him."

So when Jesus came he found that Lazarus had been in the tomb four days. Bethany was near Jerusalem about fifteen stadia away. Many of the Jews had joined the women around Martha and Mary to console them concerning their brother. Then when Martha heard that Jesus was coming she went and met him but Mary stayed in the house.

Martha said to Jesus, "Lord, if you would have been here, my brother wouldn't have died. Even now I know that whatever you ask of God, God will give you."

Jesus said to her, "Your brother will rise again."

Martha said to him, "I know that he will rise again in the resurrection of the last day."

Jesus said to her, "I am the resurrection and the life. He who believes in me will still live even if he dies. Whoever lives and believes in me will never die. Do you believe this?"

She said to him, "Yes, Lord. I have come to believe that you are the Christ, God's Son who came into the world." When she had said this, she went away and called Mary her sister saying, "The Teacher is here and wants to see you."

When Mary heard this she arose quickly and went to him. Now Jesus had not yet come into the village but was in the place where Martha met him. Then the Jews who were with Mary in the house and were consoling her saw Mary rise up quickly and went out they followed her saying, "She is going to the tomb to weep there." When Mary came to where Jesus was and when saw him, she fell down at his feet saying to him, "Lord, if you would have been here, my brother wouldn't have died."

When Jesus saw Mary and the Jews weeping He was trouble and said, "Where have you laid him?" They told him, "Lord, come and see." Jesus wept.

The Jews said, "See how much affection Jesus has for Lazarus!" Some of them said, "Couldn't this man, who opened the eyes of those who were blind, have kept this man from dying?"

Jesus came to the cave with a stone laying against it. Jesus said, "Take away the stone."

Martha said to him, "Lord, by this time there is a stench, for he has been dead four days."

Jesus said to her, "Didn't I tell you that if you believed you would see God's glory?"

So they took away the stone. Jesus lifted up his eyes and said,

"Father, thank you for listened to me. I know that you always listen to me but because of the multitude standing around I said this that they may believe that you sent me."

When Jesus said this, he cried with a loud voice, "Lazarus, come out!"Lazarus came out bound hand and foot with wrappings and his face was wrapped around with a cloth.

Jesus said to them, "Free him and let him go." Many of the Jews who came with Mary saw what Jesus did and believed in him. **John 11:1-45**

Jesus Restores Sight
As they went out from Jericho, a great multitude followed Jesus. Two blind men sitting by the road heard that Jesus was passing by cried out, "Lord, son of David have mercy on us." The multitude

rebuked them telling them that they should be quiet but they cried out even more, "Lord, son of David have mercy on us."
Jesus stop and asked, "What do you want me to do for you?"

They told him, "Lord, that our eyes may be opened."

Jesus being moved with compassion touched their eyes and immediately they could see and they followed him.
Matthew 20: 29-34, Mark 10:46-52, Luke 18: 35-43

Jesus Withers the Fig Tree
In the morning, as Jesus returned to the city and he was hungry. He saw a fig tree by the road and found nothing on it but leaves. He said to it, "Let there be no fruit from you forever!" Immediately the fig tree withered away.

The disciples said, "How did the fig tree immediately wither away?"

Jesus answered, "Most certainly I tell you, if you have faith and don't doubt you will not only do what was done to the fig tree but even if you told this mountain, 'Be taken up and cast into the sea,' it would be done. All things, whatever you ask in prayer believing you will receive." **Matthew 21:18-22, Mark 11:12-14**

Jesus Heals a Servant's Severed Ear
One of the Apostles struck the servant of the high priest and cut off his right ear.
But Jesus answered, "Let me at least do this" and he touched his ear and healed him. **Luke 22:50,51**

The Second Miraculous Catch of fish
Simon Peter said to them, "I'm going fishing."
They told him, "We are coming with you." They immediately went out and entered into the boat. That night, they caught nothing.

But when morning had come Jesus was there on the beach yet the disciples didn't know that it was Jesus. Jesus said to them, "Children, have you caught any fish?"

They answered him, "No."

He said to them, "Cast the net on the right side of the boat and you will find some fish."

They cast the net and they weren't able to draw it in for the multitude of fish. That disciple whom Jesus loved said to Peter, "It's the Lord!"

So when Peter heard that it was the Lord he wrapped his coat around himself and dove into the water. But the other disciples came in the little boat for they were not far from land dragging the net full of fish. So when they landed on land they saw a fire with fish and bread on it. Jesus said to them, "Bring some of the fish which you have just caught."
Peter went up drew the net to land full of one hundred fifty-three great fish. Even though there were so many, the net wasn't torn. **John 21:3-11**

WHO IS NORBERT J. HORNEK?

I am the writer of 10% of this book. But I did researched the last three years of the life of Jesus Christ. 90% of this book came from public domain. I used the books in the New Testament and in the Old Testament. I had this book published for for our family so they would know what God's will is.

I was born on July 24, 1935 to a Catholic family and was raised and received a Catholic education. I graduate from grade school, high school and one year of college in Louisville Kentucky. I worked in my parent's grocery store and spent 43 years in the dairy business.

In the dairy business I found out that the harder I worked the more money I could make.

I started out delivering milk to houses and stores and later I was offered and accepted a job in management. Several years later I was offered and we accepted another management job in Indianapolis, Indiana.

By this time dairies begin to struggle and the company that I was working for had to make a hard decision. Their decision was to lay off their entire sales department nation wide. I was 52 years old and now without a job. However, it wasn't long when another dairy hired me and I spent 13 years with them and a total of 43 years in the dairy business. Mary Lynne and I retired together.

I got married in 1960 to Mary Lynne Smith and we both retired in 2001. Each of our 6 living children are making a lot of money

because of their hard work at what they do. Our second child was a miscarriage and was baptist by a catholic doctor.

I created and publish this book for our children and our grand children, so they would have the knowledge of Jesus Christ and have a chance to enter the kingdom of God by doing God's will.